T0197615

THE BAD GUYS

Students/Teachers Guide to School Safety and Violence Prevention
Preschool – 3rd grade

Julie Federico

WestBow Press books may be ordered through booksellers or by contacting:

WestBow Press
A Division of Thomas Nelson
1663 Liberty Drive
Bloomington, IN 47403
www.westbowpress.com
1-(866) 928-1240

ISBN: 978-1-4497-9949-6 (sc)
ISBN: 978-1-4497-9950-2 (e)

Library of Congress Control Number: 2013911500

Printed in the United States of America.

WestBow Press rev. date: 7/2/2013

WestBow
PRESS
A DIVISION OF THOMAS NELSON

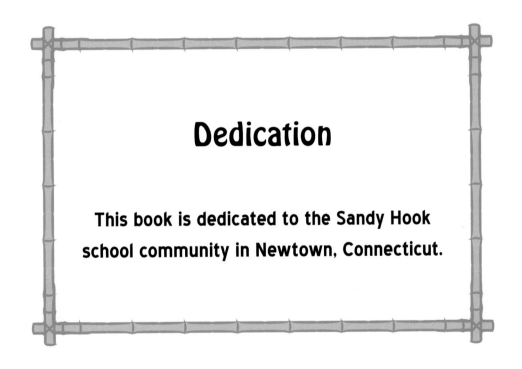

Dedication

This book is dedicated to the Sandy Hook
school community in Newtown, Connecticut.

⭐ Acknowledgement ⭐

I am grateful to Austin Eblen of West Bow Press for selecting my project and believing in my ideas. Thank you for giving me the platform to share my message with world.

A special thank you to my editors Ruth van de Witt and Brenda Von Kaenel. Thank you for taking time to edit and reedit.

I want to acknowledge my daughter Amelia Federico and her positive efforts to help me with this book. She was and is my biggest supporter and for this I am forever grateful. Not once did she say, "This is too big of a problem for you to take on. You don't even have a marketing plan." Her calm, positive, presence guided me in the direction I needed to go. She had insight into the illustrations that I did not have. Her attention to detail was phenomenal for a 10 year old. Thank you Amelia. To Olivia, who quietly played or watched another episode of _Heartland_ while I worked. How do I express my thankfulness? You contributed to this project in mighty ways as well. Your spirit is woven into this book. I love you both so much! My dream to is to make the world a safer place for children.

Schools are safe places.
Schools are places to learn
and have fun with friends.
Schools are also places
to learn table manners!

Sometimes though, schools are not safe.
Sometimes a bad guy can get inside a school.
This bad guy may want to hurt people.

How can you tell if a person is a bad guy?
Look for these clues:
    They are a stranger.
    They are running through the hallway.
    They are yelling or acting angry.
    They look unsafe or wild.

What should you do if you see someone in the hallway that you think does not belong at your school?

Quickly tell a teacher, another trusted adult, or go to the main office as soon as possible.

If a bad guy gets into a school, the principal will announce a "lockdown". Lockdown means that all students must stay inside their classrooms with the doors locked.

If you are in the bathroom or in the hallway when a lockdown starts, go to the nearest teacher right away, even if it is not your own teacher. Listen to the teacher's directions. Teachers will help keep you safe. Be completely quiet during a lockdown.

In a lockdown, the police will drive super fast to the school to help stop the bad guy.

Sometimes a kid is the bad guy. Usually
when a student wants to hurt other kids,
it is because the student was bullied for
a long time. Sometimes kids who have been
bullied may bring a gun to school.

If you hear someone say that they want to bring a gun to school, or that they want to hurt others, you must report it right away!

Tell a parent, a teacher, or call 911.

This will keep your school safer than if you do not tell anyone. This is <u>always</u> the right thing to do.

Reporting a threat does not make you a tattletale, it makes you a HERO.

You have the power to keep your school safe when you tell adults what you know to be true.

Schools are safe places; they are wonderful places
to learn and grow.
You and your friends can help make sure schools
stay safe.

Supplemental Teacher's Guide:

*You have one of the hardest jobs, please take care of yourself.

*Break these questions up over multiple days. To do them all in one day is too much. For younger grades, ask parents to come to your class when you're ready to discuss the book, so they can provide comfort to their children and reinforce key concepts at home.

*Spend a little time talking about what suspicious adults might look like and behave like.

Suspicious adults might be yelling or running through the hallway, they may be someone you have never seen before, they will probably not be wearing a District I.D. badge, they will look out of place, and they will look strange. You will know in your heart they do not belong in the building.

*When talking about safety, I would always tell my students "Students get on the bus at 6:20 am. I do not walk into the school until 7:00 am. If there is going to be a shooting, who do you think will know about it first?" They would all shout out, "We would!"

*In school shootings where the gunman was a current student, at least one student usually knew about the threat. This is very important to address. Talk about the responsibility students have to report threatening behavior. Mention that they could save other students/teachers lives with their report. Schools are usually safe; you can make them safer.

*Students have a huge responsibility to their school and community to report any information they have heard or if they become aware of a potential shooting. Stress the importance of children telling a trusted adult or law enforcement immediately. This information delivered at a critical time has the power to save lives. Students need to know that sharing their knowledge can prevent a tragedy. Even if they think the student wouldn't really do it, they should report it.

*It is hard to know what is going on inside students' heads, so after you read the book, ask:

-What did you think?

-Would you report a student who was threatening to bring a weapon to school? Why or why not?

-What should students do if they see a suspicious adult in the building?

*Have students name an adult in the building to whom they could report a threat. If students become aware of a threat outside of school hours, encourage students to call 911 with their families before school starts, rather than coming to school to make the report. Explain how important timing can be. Tell them it is important to trust their instincts. Explain what instincts are to younger children.

*Talk about erring on the side of caution, and how reporting a threat that seems real is the right thing to do even if in the end it is not true.

*Talk about what will happen to a student who reports a possible shooting which is later found to be false. Emphasize they will <u>not</u> be in trouble with law enforcement, and stress it was important they tried to help keep their school safe.

> *Talk about how students would feel if they knew of
> a threat and did not report it. What if they called in
> sick to save themselves and others were hurt? What if
> they went to school and ended up being harmed?

*Clues which demonstrate students have become saturated with the topic:

-No more questions or asking really silly, off-the-wall questions.

-Fidgety, restless behavior.

-Students try to change the subject or flat out ask you to talk about something else.

-Silence from students, or they stop making eye contact with you.

When this happens, stop the discussion and move onto something else. This is a very difficult topic; do not saturate students with information. Less is sometimes more. If students are overwhelmed or if you are overwhelmed, stop and revisit it later. Unfortunately, this topic is not going away any time soon, so do not feel you have to get through all the material in one day or one week.

I envision this book as a thread that will aid teachers throughout the year. Read it at the beginning and midway point in the school year. Use it to prepare for a lockdown drill or to foster discussions about the drill. Information such as this is better sprinkled throughout the year, because it keeps an on-going conversation happening with students. This is preferable to a large, one-day assembly where school safety is addressed and never spoken of again. I think each time you read this book to your class, you are making your school safer. I cannot think of a more important gift a school can give their students than the gift of safety.

The last section of this book is for students to write down or draw on going threats that the school should be aware of.

Remember all immediate threats should be reported to 911 as soon as possible. After you call 911, you can document your story here with details.

Draw pictures or use words to describe what happened. These details can be shared with law enforcement.

Sometimes bullies who are planning to harm students at school will send out warning threats before they act. At first these warning threats may seem casual and not something to be taken seriously.

If students write down each threat they hear from a student and the date they heard the threat, this information is very important. A list of threats will be dealt with by the school and law enforcement differently than a single threat. And several students reporting the same threat has the power to bring swift intervention.

Students should NOT take this book back to school after they have written in it. If you have written specific information in the book keep the book at home. Only take the book to school if you will be turning it into law enforcement or school officials. Only speak the real truth, write or draw what you saw, and what you heard. Your information can and will save lives.

Date_____

Date_____

Date_____

Date_____

Date_____

Date_____

Date_____

Date_____

Date_____

Date_____

Printed in the United States
By Bookmasters